CREATE THIS BOOK 2

By
Moriah Elizabeth
AND _____

(your name here)

FILL THIS EMPTY SPACE

ISBN–13: 978-0692168721

ISBN–10: 0692168729

A Little Note Before
You Get Started...

Welcome to Create This Book 2, where every page is a new creative adventure! In these pages you will find 100 prompts designed to get your creativity flowing. Feel free to modify, change and spin the directions to fit your unique style. This is YOUR creation.

If you have already completed the first Create This Book (bravo!), you may notice some differences in Create This Book 2. Some of these prompts are more open-ended. This is to give you more freedom to create! These pages may require some brainstorming, but you're a seasoned pro and you can handle it!

Be open to various ways of creating. Don't limit yourself! Remember all the options:

drawing, writing, taking photos, journaling, scrap-booking, collaging and more.

Use Imagination
try new things
personalize the prompts
Think Outside the Box
AND HAVE FUN!

Tips &

DECORATING THE FRONT/BACK COVER:

When it comes to decorating the cover, be careful with the types of media you are using to prevent smudging and splotching.

👍 BEST MATERIALS TO USE:

−Permanent Markers
(let dry completely before touching to avoid smudging)

−Acrylic Paint

−Other Decorating Materials
(stickers, gems, scrapbook paper, decorative tape, etc.)

MIXED RESULTS:

−Colored Pencils
(some brands may not be pigmented enough for even coverage)

−Crayons
. (apply easily, but may produce splotchy color)

👎 MATERIALS TO AVOID:

−Washable Markers
(prone to smudging)

−Felt Tip Pens
(prone to smudging)

−Watercolor Paint
(will not adhere properly)

Tricks

DECORATING THE INTERIOR:

The pages in this book are a little thin, but we can work around that (after all, we all are creative people here!).

 **BEST MATERIALS TO USE:**

–Pens

–Acrylic Paint

–Pencils & Colored Pencils

–Crayons

–Chalk & Charcoal

–Other Decorating Materials
(stickers, gems, scrapbook paper, decorative tape, etc.)

TO USE WET MEDIA (markers, watercolor paint, etc.)

If you want to use wet media on certain pages, no problem! To prevent bleeding through the paper, use wet media on a separate piece of paper and glue your finished artwork into the book. OR glue a blank sheet of paper into the book first, trim the edges, and then create on top. **You can even cut a window in the paper so you can still see the directions.**

PROTECT YOUR ARTWORK!

To preserve your artwork and keep it neat, try applying a matte clear coat over top, or use clear packing tape to cover your art.

To see a video tutorial of these TIPS & TRICKS, check out Moriah Elizabeth's Create This Book 2 introduction video on YouTube.

Create a
fresh
start

Beginning Date:

May (Tue) 4th (6:00)

My Goals for This Book:

_____

_____

_____

_____

Create *confetti*

Make confetti by cutting
small pieces of paper
(or other materials).
Glue it onto this page.

CREATE
a page of
Lyrics

**Write the lyrics
to a song(s) here.**

CREATE A COMPARISON

USE COLORS
YOU LOVE
on this page.

USE COLORS
YOU DISLIKE
on this page.

CREATE A **merge**

Choose two animals.
Merge them together.

CREATE integration

Integrate O this line into
a design or drawing.

_____

CREAT A PUZZLE

Turn this page into a puzzle

CREATE
an assortment

Fill in each box with
something different.

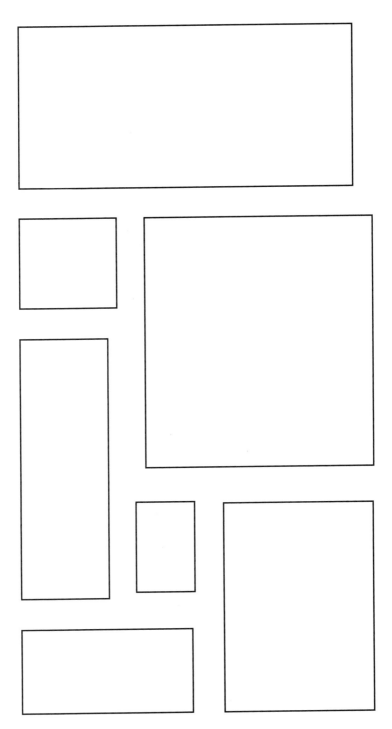

create WORD *illustration*

Incorporate illustration into a word to show its meaning.

Example: Write the word "hot" and add flames to the lettering

Create a List of
FAVORITES

Choose any category (places, movies, foods, etc.)
make a list of all your favorites.

MY FAVORITE : _____

(CHOSEN CATEGORY)

Create randoMness

scatter random things all over this page.

create *Shine* ✳

Figure out a way to make this page shiny.

CREATE A
SELF-PORTRAIT

Make a list of things
that make you, "you."

CREATE AN

Make your own invention. Draw the diagrams for it here.

INVENTION

Create a Reminder
Write something you should always remember.

CREATE a scented page
Use this page to capture your favorite scent(s).

CREATE A
PAGE
PAGE

Tear a page from an old book or magazine.
Stick it onto this page.
Find a way to make it more interesting
(cut it up, write over it, incorporate
it into a drawing etc.).

CREATE color

Make different colors by mixing paint. Give each color a creative name.

CREATE Beauty out of ugliness

Choose something you think is ugly. Find a way to make it beautiful.

CREATE
ugliness
out of
beauty

**Choose something
you think is
beautiful.
Find a way to
make it ugly.**

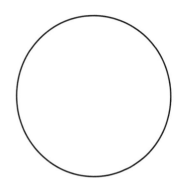

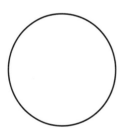

CREATE
ADDITIONS
Add to these circles.

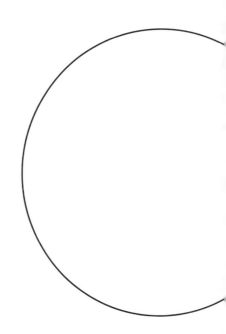

Create a Status

I am feeling:

create a
CHARACTER

fill out the following blanks at random
or ask a friend to fill them for you.

Adjective: _____

Color: _____

Animal: _____

Compile the 3 answers to create a
unique character. Draw him or her here.

create a
mini book

Use the template to create a mini book.

1. Rip out page 53

2. Cut out each of the 3 rectangles
(along the black lines).

3. Fold each piece in half (on the center gray line).

4. Stack the pieces on top of one another and attach
them on the folded line by stapling, sewing or gluing.

**Write and/or illustrate your mini book
on a topic of your choice!**

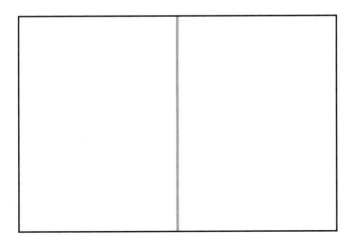

**Once complete, glue the back cover of
your mini book onto this page to display it.**

CREATE DRIPS

create on black...

create a day dream

Allow yourself to
daydream here.

CREATE
ACTIVITY

Dedicate this page to your
favorite sport or activity
by filling it with drawings,
writing, and/or photos.

CREATE
HAND PRINTS
Place your hand prints here.

CREATE string decor

Decorate these
pages using pieces
of string, thread or yarn.

CREATE
— A —
DESIGN

What is something you have always wanted to design? Now is your chance!

Design your own:

_____

examples: house, clothing, character, store etc.

CREATE
SADNESS

Make this page sad.

CREATE A

~~SPLIT~~
DECISION

**Write or draw
the first thing that
comes to mind.**

create
a wish

Make a wish here.

CREATE A MODIFIED CHARACTER

Choose an existing character.
Draw him/her with ONE modification.
(change color, remove part of costume, etc.)

create
INCOMPLETION

Start drawing something on
this page. Never finish it.

CREATE contrast

WRITE ABOUT THE *high* **POINT OF YOUR DAY:**

WRITE ABOUT THE *Low* **POINT OF YOUR DAY:**

CREATE A LINE

Decorate this page using a long, continuous line.

 # CREATE

a re-purposing

Give bits of wrappers and/or packaging a new purpose on this page.

create
seasonal
DECOR

Decorate this page
based on the current season.

create whatever.

Use this page to create
ANYTHING you want.

create bleed

Use markers or paint and let the colors bleed through the page.

CREATE A BORDER

Cut a border around this page by cutting shapes out of the edges.

CREATE
a *dream* journal

Document a dream.

CREATE softness

Make this page soft.

create AN inventory

(Of Things You Own)

SOMETHING **OLD:** _____

SOMETHING **NEW:** _____

SOMETHING **UGLY:** _____

SOMETHING **CUTE:** _____

SOMETHING **HANDMADE:** _____

SOMETHING **GIFTED:** _____

SOMETHING **BROKEN:** _____

SOMETHING **THRIFTED:** _____

CREATE

splatter

Splatter paint here.

CREATE
layers

Make this page layered by adding bits of paper, tape, ribbon, stickers etc.

create a question

use this page
to ask a question.

CREATE A
historical reference

Write about or draw pictures
of any historical event or figure.

create a makeover.

**Find something that could use some improvement.
Give it a makeover.**

AFTER

CREATE A
COLORFUL
PAGE

Create a To Do List.

CREATE a comic strip

Use these boxes to make your own comic.

create
a miracle

Make the impossible, POSSIBLE.

create
cuteness

CREATE
DISSENTION
Record popular trends or current fads you don't like.

CREATE
A MESS

Get messy on this page!

create
reflection

Dedicate this page to your past self.
Fill it with things you would have liked.

create
color
temperature

Use warm colors on this page (red, orange, yellow).

Use cool colors on this page (green, blue, purple).

create
→ **EMPHASIS**

Place multiple things on this page.
Choose ONE of them to emphasize
using color, size, lines etc.

Create
an alphabet

Write every letter of
the alphabet on this page.

create a
REPAIR

1. Crumple, rip, cut and/or stain this page (or have a friend do it for you).

2. Try to repair the damage.

Create
Imitation
Recreate a famous
piece of artwork.

CREATE
A PASTEL PAGE

Use only light colors on this page.

CREATE | A | SERIES

Display a series here (real or fantasy).

CREATE A SHOCK

Do something unexpected
by decorating this page in
an uncharacteristic way (use
techniques, imagery, etc.
that you don't usually use).

CREATE a room

Design this room by coloring the walls, filling it with furniture and/or adding windows.

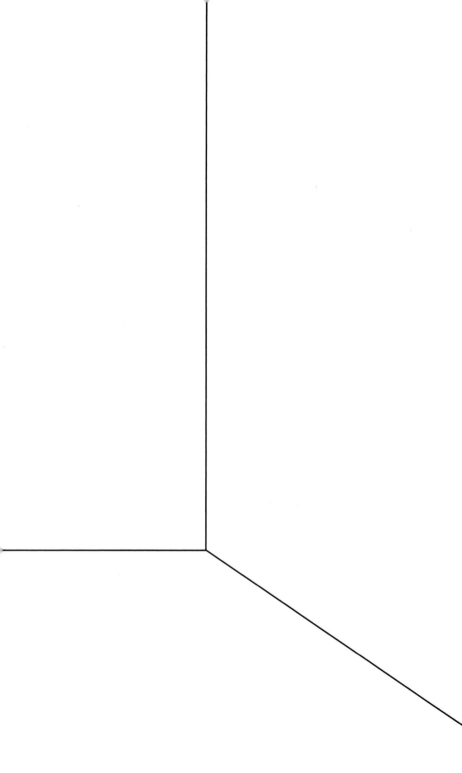

create
animal
PRINTS

CREATE
a difference in altitude

ON THIS PAGE:
Display something you find underwater.

ON THIS PAGE:
Display something you find in the sky.

create a mystery

Hide something in
or on this page.

create
vAriety
Include as many different
colors, textures and/or
materials on this page.

CREATE
a pedestal

Put something unusual on this pedestal.

CREATE

CONFUSION

Make
this
page
difficult
to
understand.

create peace

Make this page as peaceful as possible.

create
assemblage

Write or draw something on a separate sheet of paper. Cut it up and reassemble it on this page **in a different way than you made it originally.**

create
a theme

Decorate this page
based on a theme.

create
repetition
repetition
repetition

Fill this space by repeating something over and over.

CREATE
positivity

Fill this page with positivity.

create
negativity

Fill this page with negativity.

CREATE
modern art
Challenge the meaning of art.

create
a new prompt

Choose two pages in this book.

Combine their instructions to form

a completely new prompt.

page # _____ **AND** **page #** _____

```
new prompt:



```

create
disproportion
Draw or collage an image with distorted proportions.

CREATE
A NEON PAGE

Use neon colors on this page.

CREATE
disorientation

Place the open book in front of you on a flat surface. SPIN IT! Decorate this page using whatever angle it lands in.

create
A PERSONAL
CHALLENGE

Use this page to try an art
form you find difficult.

CREATE
a dichotomy

1. Carefully draw neat outlines for any kind of image.

2. Color the drawing carelessly, disregarding neatness entirely.

CREATE
an activity log

Make a list of activities you do on
a regular basis (at least once a week).

create a list of

pet peeves

write down your top
10 worst pet peeves.

CREATE
a recreation

Find a photo, drawing or piece of writing from when you were younger. Recreate it here.

Option 1: Improve your old work

Option 2: Replicate your old work as closely as possible

create a
TRANSLATION

Write one word in different languages.

CREATE
A LIMITATION

Gather a box of art supplies.
Close your eyes and choose 3 at random.
Use only those 3 to complete this page.

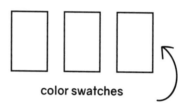

color swatches

CREATE
DOCUMENTATION

Document one of your current belongings by writing about it, drawing it, or attaching photos of it on this page.

create a
KNIFE
painting

paint a picture using a plastic knife.

CREATE
Unexpected
COLOR

Change something that is black & white into something that is full of color!

create an
ALTERATION

Choose something you hate.
Figure out how to make it more appealing.

CREATE AN OFFICIAL END

FINISHING DATE:

_____